Et Voilà!

Pupil's Book 1

Chris Johnson

Head of Languages
Counthill School, Oldham

Illustrated by
Ted Andrews

HODDER AND STOUGHTON

LONDON SYDNEY AUCKLAND TORONTO

Acknowledgements

The author and publishers wish to thank the following for their kind permission to reproduce photographs: Aerofilms, Aéroport de Paris, Air France, Air UK, British Hovercraft Corporation, Citroën Cars Ltd, Commissariat Général du Tourism, French Government Tourist Office, Keith Gibson, Topham.

Cover photographs: Peter Downes and Keith Gibson.

British Library Cataloguing in Publication Data
Johnson, Christopher
  Et Voilà!
  1. Pupils' book
  1. French language – Text-books
  I. Title
  448.2'421   PC2112
  ISBN 0 340 24949 8

Third impression 1986

Copyright © 1983 Chris Johnson. All rights reserved. No part of this publication may be reproduced or transmitted in any form or by any means, electronic or mechanical, including photocopy, recording, or any information storage and retrieval system, without permission in writing from the publisher.

Typeset in Optima (VIP) by Macmillan India Ltd., Bangalore

Printed for Hodder and Stoughton Educational, a division of Hodder and Stoughton Ltd, Mill Road, Dunton Green, Sevenoaks, Kent, by Colorcraft Ltd, Hong Kong.

Contents

1 A la douane   1

2 Dans la rue   11

3 Au camping   21

4 Au bureau de tabac   31

5 Au syndicat d'initiative   41

6 Au café 1   51

Je vous présente...

LA FAMILLE RAGOUT

Voici **Monsieur Ragoût**.

Il travaille dans un restaurant à Londres.

Voici **Madame Ragoût**.

Elle est secrétaire.

Voici **Monique Ragoût**.

Elle adore la musique pop.

Voici **Jacques Ragoût**.

Il adore le football.

UNIT ONE — A LA DOUANE

A. DIALOGUE

The Ragoût family have left London, where they live, to have a camping holiday in their home-country of France. Having crossed the Channel, they drive through the customs.

1.

Douanier: Vous avez trois valises, monsieur?

2.

M. Ragoût: Oui! J'ai aussi un sac à dos.

3.

M. Ragoût: Et voici mon sac de voyage...

4.

M. Ragoût: ... et ma serviette.

5.

Douanier: Ah! Vous avez quelque chose à déclarer?

6.

M. Ragoût: J'ai une bouteille de whisky!

7.

Douanier: Oh, ça va! Passez!

8.

M. Ragoût: Merci, monsieur!

9.

Douanier: Bonnes vacances!

B. USEFUL WORDS

un sac à dos un sac de voyage une serviette
un sac à main une valise un panier

C. WHAT CAN YOU SPOT?

Look carefully at the picture! It shows the house where the Ragoût family live in London. Do you know how to say in French any of the things shown on it? As well as the new words you have learnt in this unit, you will probably be able to find a number of words that you know already. Write a list of these words and see who can make the longest list!

D. LOOK WHAT I'VE GOT!

Look down the list of words you made under **C.** and see how many of these things you actually have yourself. Now make up a sentence in French about each one.

N.B. Make sure your teacher has checked that you have got the correct spellings first, and copy the words very carefully!

Example
J'ai un sac à dos.

E. WHAT I HAVEN'T GOT!

Look at the picture and your list of words once more. This time find the things you have **not** got. Again make up sentences about each one, trying to make as many as possible.

Example
Je n'ai pas de sac à main.

F. ASKING THE QUESTIONS

How would you ask someone if they have the things shown in the pictures?

Example
Vous avez un panier?

G. HAVE YOU, OR HAVEN'T YOU?

Write down in French the answers to these questions about yourself.

Example

Question: Vous avez un sac à dos?

Answers: Oui, j'ai un sac à dos.

or: Non, je n'ai pas de sac à dos.

1. Vous avez un sac à main?
2. Vous avez un stylo?
3. Vous avez une maison?
4. Vous avez une table?
5. Vous avez une valise?
6. Vous avez un sac de voyage?
7. Vous avez un chien?
8. Vous avez un panier?
9. Vous avez un crayon?
10. Vous avez une serviette?

H. IT'S MINE!

Work out what the person is saying in each of these pictures. The word for **my** must be included in each one.

with **un** words = **mon**

with **une** words = **ma**

I. WHAT WOULD YOU SAY?

How would you cope with the French customs? Imagine that you are the holiday-maker in the pictures. What would the customs officer say to you, and what would you say in reply? You should not find it too difficult if you follow the pattern of the original dialogue.

J. STORY TIME
Les biscuits de Toto
Part 1

Mlle Lemoine est très riche! Elle a quatre maisons, un yacht, cinq autos et un avion! Elle adore les chiens. Son chien favori est Toto – c'est un petit pékinois brun.

Un jour Mlle Lemoine décide de dîner au restaurant. Elle arrive devant le restaurant dans une voiture noire. Charles, son chauffeur, ouvre la porte de la voiture et elle entre dans le restaurant avec Toto. Elle porte un sac à main blanc.

Questions
1. What kind of person is Mlle Lemoine?
2. Give details of all the things she owns.
3. What is she very fond of?
4. Who is Toto?
5. Describe Toto.
6. What does she decide to do one day?
7. How does she get there?
8. Who is Charles?
9. What does he do when they arrive?
10. What does Mlle Lemoine do?
11. What is she carrying?

Part 2

Dans le restaurant, un homme regarde Mlle Lemoine. Il est sur une chaise, devant le bar. Soudain, il saisit le sac à main de Mlle Lemoine. Il quitte le restaurant et monte dans une voiture bleue.

Mlle Lemoine crie: 'Mon sac à main! Mon sac à main!'

Un agent de police arrive, mais l'homme a disparu!

Dix minutes après, l'homme entre dans sa maison et ouvre le sac à main. Dans le sac il y a une boîte. Il ouvre la boîte. Et qu'est-ce qu'il y a dans la boîte? Des perles? Non! Des diamants? Non! Il y a des biscuits pour le chien Toto!

Questions
1. What is the man in the restaurant doing?
2. Where exactly in the restaurant is he?
3. What does he do suddenly?
4. How does he make his getaway?
5. What does Mlle Lemoine do?
6. Who arrives?
7. What has happened to the man?
8. How long does it take the man to get to his house?
9. What does he find in the handbag at first?
10. What two things does he hope might be inside?
11. What in fact has he stolen from Mlle Lemoine?

K. FIND OUT FOR YOURSELF

Photo quiz

1. The most popular way of getting to France is of course by boat, using one of the many ferry routes available. There are, however, other ways of making the crossing and these photos show you two alternative forms of cross-channel transport.

Now see if you can find out the answers to the following questions.

a. From which English ports or airports do they leave and which towns do they go to in France?
b. How long do the crossings take?
c. Are these two ways of crossing the channel cheaper or more expensive than going by boat?

An interview

2. Find someone who has been to France (relative, friend, teacher) and interview him or her about the journey, using the following questions:

a. Did you go by boat/hovercraft/plane?
b. Was it
   French or English?
   old or new?
   very comfortable, quite comfortable or uncomfortable?
   very crowded, quite crowded or fairly empty?
   clean or dirty?
c. From which English port/airport did you leave?
d. At which French port/airport did you arrive?
e. How long did the crossing take?
f. Was it calm or rough?
g. What did you do during the crossing?
h. Did you come back the same way?

UNIT TWO — DANS LA RUE

A. DIALOGUES

1. The Ragoût family have just arrived in Beauport where they are to spend their holiday. They have parked the car and are standing at the corner of boulevard de Paris and rue Victor Hugo. Mme Ragoût wants to post a letter at once, so she asks a policeman the way to the post office.

2. Monsieur Ragoût is more concerned about finding the campsite. While his wife is posting her letter, he stops a lady and asks her how to get there.

1.
Mme Ragoût: Pardon, monsieur l'agent!
Agent de Police: Oui, madame?

2.
Mme Ragoût: Pour aller à la Poste, s'il vous plaît?

3.
Agent de Police: Prenez cette rue jusqu'à la boulangerie.
Mme Ragoût: Oui.

4.
Agent de Police: Tournez à droite.

5.
Agent de Police: Traversez la place. La Poste est à gauche.

6.
Mme Ragoût: Merci beaucoup, monsieur!
Agent de Police: Je vous en prie, madame!

1.
M. Ragoût: Pardon, madame!
Femme: Oui, monsieur?

2.
M. Ragoût: Pour aller au camping, s'il vous plaît?

3.
Femme: Prenez cette rue jusqu'au syndicat d'initiative.
M. Ragoût: Oui.

4.
Femme: Tournez à gauche.

5.
Femme: Traversez le pont. Le camping est à droite.

6.
M. Ragoût: Merci beaucoup, madame!
Femme: Je vous en prie, monsieur!

B. USEFUL WORDS

la boulangerie	la plage	le commissariat
la boucherie	la place du marché	le stade
la pâtisserie	le supermarché	le camping
la Poste	le bureau de tabac	le syndicat d'initiative
la banque	le restaurant	l'épicerie
la piscine	le café	l'église

C. ASKING THE WAY

The people in these pictures want to get to a number of different places in the town. Work out where they want to go to and how they should ask the way there. The places in these first pictures are all **la** words.

Example

Pour aller **à la** poste, s'il vous plaît?

The places in these pictures are all **le** words.

Example

Pour aller **au** camping, s'il vous plaît?

D. LEFT OR RIGHT

Look at the picture and find out whether the places you are asked about are on the left or on the right. Then answer the questions using either **à gauche** or **à droite**.

Example

Question: Où est la plage?
Answer: A droite.

1. Où est le café?
2. Où est la Poste?
3. Où est l'épicerie?
4. Où est la piscine?
5. Où est le commissariat?
6. Où est l'église?
7. Où est la boulangerie?
8. Où est le stade?
9. Où est la place du marché?
10. Où est le camping?
11. Où est le syndicat d'initiative?
12. Où est la boucherie?

E. FOLLOW THE TRAIL

Follow these directions on the street map of Beauport and see where they end up. Make a note of where each trail ends, but do not tell anybody else – it will spoil their fun!

1. **Départ: le camping.** Prenez l'avenue de la Mer jusqu'au bureau de tabac. Tournez à gauche. Prenez la rue Victor Hugo jusqu'au commissariat. Tournez à droite. _____ est à gauche.
2. **Départ: l'église.** Prenez l'avenue Charles de Gaulle jusqu'à la rue du Marché. Tournez à droite. Traversez le pont. Tournez à droite. _____ est à gauche.
3. **Départ: la boucherie.** Prenez le boulevard Pompidou jusqu'au supermarché. Tournez à droite. Prenez l'avenue Napoléon jusqu'à la place de la Gare. Tournez à gauche. Traversez la place. _____ est à gauche.
4. **Départ: la place du Marché.** Prenez le boulevard Pompidou jusqu'à la boucherie. Tournez à droite. Prenez la rue Victor Hugo jusqu'à l'avenue Charles de Gaulle. Tournez à droite. _____ est à droite.
5. **Départ: le stade.** Prenez le boulevard de Paris jusqu'à la boulangerie. Tournez à gauche. Prenez l'avenue Napoléon jusqu'à la piscine. Tournez à gauche. _____ est à droite.

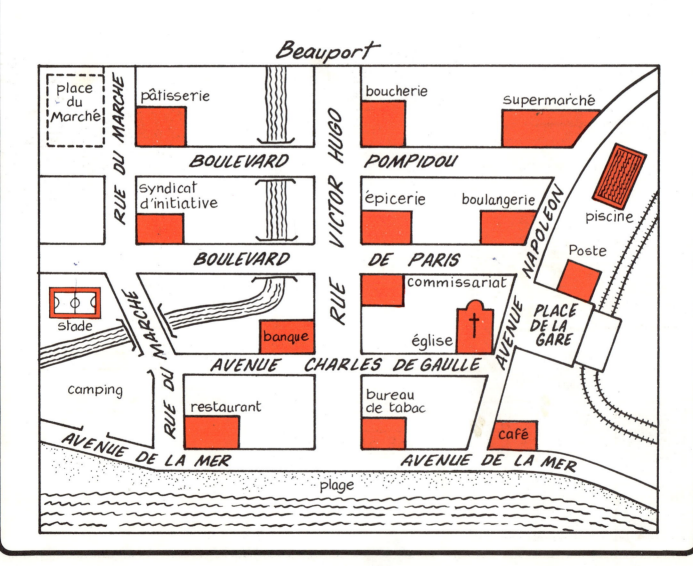

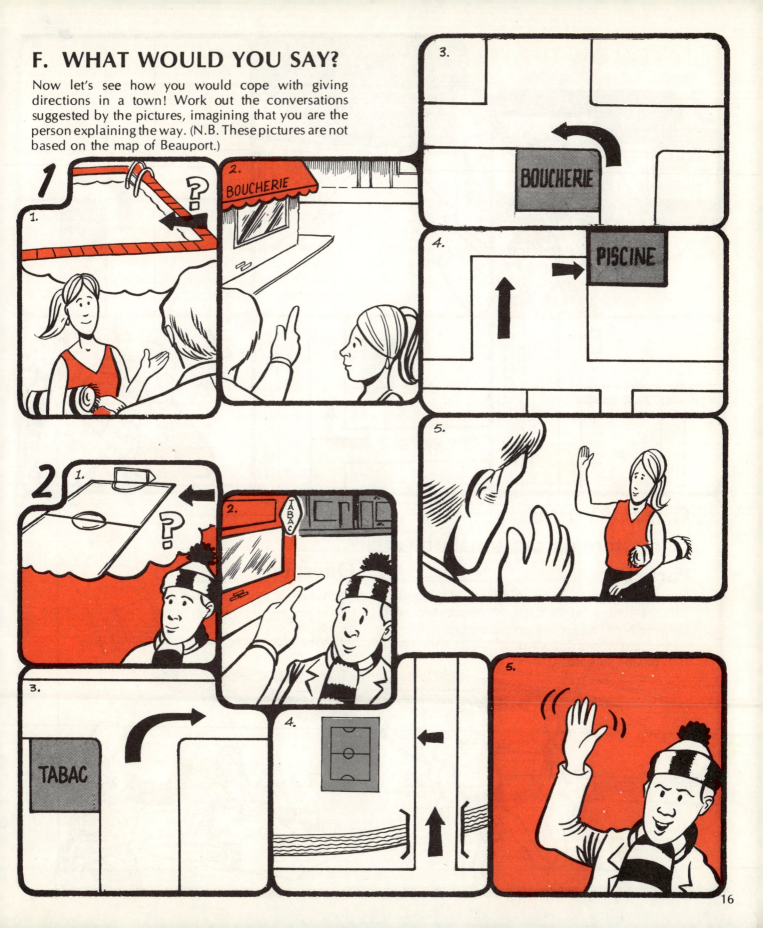

G. STORY TIME

Le mystère du sac à main bleu

Part 1

La famille Ragoût est sur la plage. M. Ragoût et Jacques jouent au football. Monique écoute la radio et Mme Ragoût lit un magazine.

Soudain Mme Ragoût dit: 'Ah les tomates! Je n'ai pas de tomates!'

Questions

1. Where is the Ragoût family?
2. What are the various members of the family doing?
3. What does Mme Ragoût suddenly realise?

Elle prend son panier et son sac à main et dit: 'Au revoir! Je vais au marché!'

Mme Ragoût prend l'avenue de la Mer jusqu'au restaurant. Elle tourne à droite et prend la rue du Marché. Quand elle arrive au marché elle achète un kilo de tomates et deux kilos d'oranges. Elle pose les tomates et les oranges dans son panier. Puis elle prend le boulevard Pompidou jusqu'à la rue Victor Hugo. Mme Ragoût tourne à droite, traverse la rue et entre dans l'épicerie. Elle achète un paquet de café et deux paquets de biscuits. Elle quitte l'épicerie et retourne à la plage.

Part 2

Soudain Mme Ragoût s'écrie: 'Mon sac à main! Je n'ai pas mon sac à main! Il a disparu!'

Mme Ragoût cherche le sac à main dans la rue Victor Hugo, mais il n'est pas là. Elle entre dans l'épicerie et demande: 'Vous avez trouvé un sac à main?' Mais la réponse est: 'Non!'

Enfin Mme Ragoût décide d'aller au commissariat. Elle entre et dit: 'J'ai perdu mon sac à main. Il est bleu. Dans le sac à main il y a mon passeport et 500 francs!'

L'agent de police répond: 'J'ai deux sacs à main blancs, quatre sacs à main noirs, et un sac à main beige, mais je n'ai pas de sac à main bleu!'

4. What two things does she take with her?
5. Where is she going?
6. What route does Mme Ragoût follow?
7. Which two items does she buy?
8. Where does she put the things she buys?

9. What two things does she do when she reaches rue Victor Hugo?
10. Which shop does she go into first?
11. What does she buy there?
12. What does she do when she comes out of the shop?

Questions

1. What dreadful discovery does Mme Ragoût make?
2. Where does she start her search?
3. Where does she go next?
4. What is the third place that she goes to?
5. What colour is the object that she is looking for?
6. What is inside it?
7. What does the policeman say in reply?

Part 3

Mme Ragoût quitte le commissariat et prend l'avenue Victor Hugo en direction de la plage. Elle pense: 'Quel désastre pour les vacances! Il faut retourner à Londres!'

Mme Ragoût ouvre un paquet de biscuits et commence à manger un biscuit. Mais soudain elle remarque quelque chose de bleu dans son panier. C'est son sac à main – sous le café et les biscuits! Mme Ragoût pousse un cri de joie: 'Je suis sauvée!' Et pour célébrer cela elle mange encore un biscuit. Hmm! Délicieux!

Questions

1. What does Mme Ragoût do when she comes out of the police station?
2. How will their holiday be affected now?
3. What does she do next?
4. What does she notice in her basket?
5. What does it turn out to be?
6. Where exactly is it?
7. What is Mme Ragoût's reaction?
8. What does she do to celebrate?

H. FIND OUT FOR YOURSELF

What do you know about the geography of France? Here is a photo quiz to test your knowledge. You may even learn something new!

These photographs either show, or have something to do with, a number of well-known places in France. You are given a little information about them, but you are not told which the places are. It is your job to find out!

Below is a list of the correct answers, but you have to work out which pictures they go with. You can use an atlas, an encyclopaedia or other books, or else you can ask people who might know the answers. Happy hunting!

| Alps | Loire | Strasbourg | Nice |
| Paris | Marseille | Toulouse | |

1. This island is the ancient heart of one of Europe's biggest cities. Name the city.

2. Mont Blanc, Europe's highest mountain. In which range of mountains is it to be found?

3. The largest town on the French Riviera. What is it called?

4. The Anglo-French 'Concorde'. In which town was it made in France?

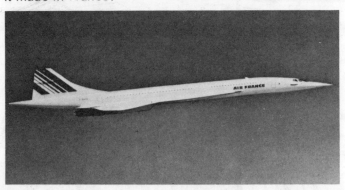

5. One of the beautiful 'châteaux' for which the valley of one of the main rivers of France is famous. What is the river called?

6. This large port on the Mediterranean gave its name to the French national anthem. Name the port.

7. An old town near the German border, now the seat of the European Parliament. Name the town.

1.
M. Ragoût: Bonjour, monsieur! Vous avez des emplacements libres?

2.
Gardien: Certainement, monsieur!

3.
M. Ragoût: C'est combien par personne?

4.
Gardien: Cinq francs par nuit.

5.
M. Ragoût: Et pour l'emplacement?

6.
Gardien: Trois francs cinquante, et deux francs cinquante pour la voiture.

7.
M. Ragoût: Ah bon! Où sont les douches, s'il vous plaît?

8.
Gardien: Dans le bloc sanitaire...

9.
Gardien: ...à côté de la piscine.

10.
M. Ragoût: Et où est l'alimentation?

11.
Gardien: Là-bas, en face du café.

12.
M. Ragoût: Merci, monsieur!

B. USEFUL WORDS

un emplacement
le bureau
le bloc sanitaire

l'alimentation
les toilettes
les douches

les lavabos
les bacs à vaisselle

D. TELL ME WHERE!

In the picture you can see Monique and Jacques studying the plan of a campsite. It is not the one where they are staying, so they do not know their way around. Answer their questions by telling them what each place is next to or opposite.

Use **à côté** or **en face**, followed by:

with a **le** word – **du**
with a **la** word – **de la**
with a **l'** word – **de l'**

Example

Question: Où est le café?
Answer: A côté **de l'**alimentation.

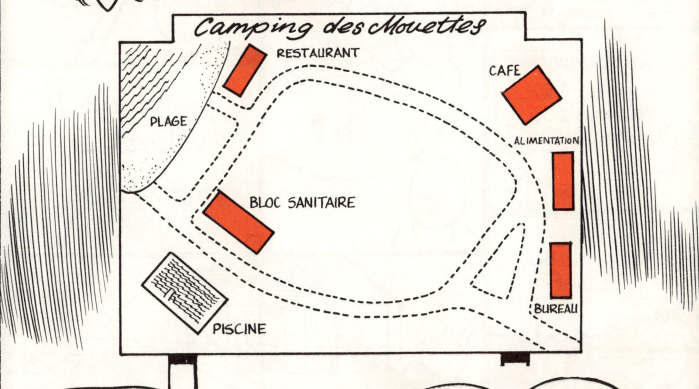

1. Où est le bloc sanitaire?
2. Où est le bureau?
3. Où est le restaurant?
4. Où est la piscine?
5. Où est l'alimentation?

E. WHAT WOULD YOU SAY?

Now it's your turn! You should know enough by now to make yourself understood when you reach a French campsite. Imagine that you are the camper, and work out from the pictures the conversation that would take place between you and the campsite warden.

F. STORY TIME
Les dangers du whisky!
Part 1

En arrivant au camping les Ragoût installent leur tente – c'est une grande tente orange – dans les dunes en face de la plage. M. Ragoût gare la voiture – une Renault bleue – à droite de la tente. Puis il prépare une omelette délicieuse (c'est sa spécialité!), et pour célébrer leur arrivée on boit une bouteille de champagne. Tout le monde est content.

Questions

1. What kind of tent has the Ragoût family got?
2. Where do they pitch it?
3. What kind of car have they got?
4. Where does M. Ragoût park it?
5. What do they eat and drink for their evening meal?

'Ah! La vue est magnifique!' dit Mme Ragoût.

A huit heures M. Ragoût dit: 'Au revoir' à sa famille et quitte le camping. Il prend l'avenue de la Mer jusqu'au bureau de tabac, tourne à gauche et entre dans un petit café en face du commissariat. Il commande un grand whisky et s'assied à une table à gauche de la porte.

6. What does Mme Ragoût admire?
7. What does M. Ragoût do at eight o'clock?
8. Describe his route and say where he ends up.
9. Describe the position of the place he goes into.
10. What does he order and where does he sit?

Part 2

Cinq minutes après un homme entre.

M. Ragoût s'écrie: 'André! Ce n'est pas possible!'

Mais oui, c'est André Leflic, son ancien camarade de classe.

L'homme regarde M. Ragoût et dit: 'Georges! Quelle coïncidence!'

M. Leflic commande un Pernod et s'assied à côté de M. Ragoût. Il explique qu'il est maintenant inspecteur de police à Beauport. M. Ragoût explique qu'il est en vacances à Beauport avec sa famille. Les deux hommes ont une longue conversation. M. Ragoût boit beaucoup de whisky et M. Leflic boit beaucoup de Pernod.

A onze heures M. Ragoût dit 'Au revoir' à M. Leflic et quitte le café pour retourner au camping. Après quatre whiskys il est très gai, mais il marche avec difficulté. Il entre en collision avec un lampadaire et dit: 'Oh, pardon, madame!'.

Questions

1. How long is it before the man comes in?
2. Who is the man?
3. What does the man say?
4. What does he order and where does he sit?
5. What does he explain to M. Ragoût?
6. What does M. Ragoût explain to him?
7. What happens after that?
8. At what time do they both leave the café?
9. What kind of state is M. Ragoût in, and what is the reason for this?
10. What incident happens on the way back to the campsite?

Part 3

Enfin M. Ragoût arrive au camping et cherche sa tente.

'Ah, voilà!' dit-il, et il s'avance vers une tente orange à côté d'une voiture bleue. Dans la tente il fait très noir, mais il voit une femme sur un lit de camping.

'Ah, ma pauvre femme,' pense M. Ragoût, 'elle est si fatiguée!'

Il embrasse la femme et dit: 'Bonne nuit, Françoise!'

Soudain la femme se lève et pousse un cri de terreur. 'Au secours! Police! Il y a un homme dans ma tente!'

Ce n'est pas Mme Ragoût, c'est une autre femme!

'Mon Dieu!' pense M. Ragoût, j'ai fait une erreur! Ce n'est pas ma femme! Ce n'est pas ma tente!'

Immédiatement il quitte la tente et disparaît dans la nuit.

Questions

1. What does M. Ragoût do on arriving at the campsite?
2. What makes him think he is in the right place?
3. What does he see inside the tent?
4. What does he think?
5. What does he do?
6. What does he say?
7. What does the lady do all of a sudden?
8. What does she shout out?
9. What does M. Ragoût realise?
10. What does he do?

G. FIND OUT FOR YOURSELF

If you go to France on holiday you should not be at a loss for things to see. Here are pictures of places which are much visited by tourists, together with a little information about each one. The names of the places are given in the list, but your job is to work out which pictures they go with. If you look up the names in an encyclopaedia or other reference book you should soon find out the answers.

Avignon   Le Puy
Bayeux   Lourdes
Chenonceaux   Monte Carlo
Mont St Michel   Versailles
Pont du Gard

1. Strictly speaking this Riviera town is not in France. It is part of a French-speaking state ruled over by a prince. It is famous for its Casino and its car rally.

2. Part of a tapestry telling the story of William the Conqueror's invasion of England in 1066. It was made by his wife, Queen Matilda, and is named after the town in Normandy where it is on display.

3. This is perhaps the most beautiful of all the châteaux in the area of the River Loire. It is known as the 'Château of Six Women' and is built across the entire width of the River Cher (which runs into the Loire).

4. What a place to build a church! It is perched on a pinnacle of volcanic rock in an old town in the southern Massif Central. Pilgrims used to climb up to it on their knees. Name the town.

5. The remains of a famous bridge over the River Rhône. According to the well known song this was a favourite spot for dancing! In the town one can also visit the palace where the Popes lived for a hundred years.

6. The Romans built this bridge as an aqueduct to supply the town of Nîmes with fresh water. It has stood for two thousand years in spite of being constructed entirely of dry stone without any cement or mortar.

7. A sumptuous palace built at enormous expense by Louis XIV, the 'Sun King', just outside Paris. The gardens are enormous and there is even a small artificial village which was very popular with the unfortunate Marie Antoinette.

8. Every year thousands of sick people flock to this town in the foothills of the Pyrenees. They come seeking a miracle cure in the waters of the grotto where, 120 years ago, Saint Bernadette had a vision of the Virgin Mary.

9. This is a tiny rocky island off the coast of Normandy and Brittany. It is linked to the mainland only by a narrow causeway and is crowned by a magnificent abbey which is over 500 years old.

UNIT FOUR

AU BUREAU DE TABAC

A. DIALOGUE

After a few days in Beauport, Jacques decides to write to some of his friends. He therefore goes into a **bureau de tabac** to buy some postcards and some stamps.

1. **Vendeuse:** Bonjour, monsieur, vous désirez?

2. **Jacques:** C'est combien les cartes postales, s'il vous plaît?

3. **Vendeuse:** Un franc trente et un franc quarante.

4. **Jacques:** Je voudrais cinq cartes postales à un franc trente.

5. **Vendeuse:** Voilà, monsieur!

6. **Jacques:** Vous avez des timbres?

7. **Vendeuse:** Oui, monsieur.

8. **Jacques:** Je voudrais cinq timbres à un franc vingt.

9. **Vendeuse:** Voilà, monsieur! C'est tout?

10. **Jacques:** Oui, merci. Ça fait combien?
    Vendeuse: Ça fait douze francs cinquante.

11. **Jacques:** Voilà, madame!
    Vendeuse: Merci, monsieur.

12. **Jacques:** Au revoir, madame!
    Vendeuse: Au revoir, monsieur!

B. USEFUL WORDS

des cartes postales	une carte postale	un paquet d'enveloppes
des timbres	un timbre	un paquet de bonbons
des journaux	un journal	un paquet de cigarettes
des magazines	un magazine	une boîte d'allumettes
des enveloppes	une enveloppe	
des bonbons	un bonbon	
des cigarettes	une cigarette	
des allumettes	une allumette	

C. HAVE YOU GOT ANY...?

You go into a shop hoping to buy the things shown in the pictures.

a. How would you ask if the shopkeeper has any?

b. Look at the picture of the shop and see if these things are in stock. Then try to work out what the shopkeeper would say in answer to your questions.

Example

a. *Your question*: 'Vous avez des cartes postales?'

b. *Shopkeeper's reply*: 'Oui, j'ai des cartes postales'.

or: 'Non, je n'ai pas de cartes postales'.

D. OWN UP!

Now it is your turn to be quizzed! Say whether or not you have got the things you are asked about. Answer in French, and don't forget – tell the truth!
The answers will begin:

Either: 'Oui, j'ai des . . . .'
or: 'Non, je n'ai pas de . . . ./Non je n'ai pas d' . . . .'

1. Vous avez des bonbons?
2. Vous avez des cartes postales?
3. Vous avez des livres?
4. Vous avez des cigarettes?
5. Vous avez des stylos?
6. Vous avez des journaux?
7. Vous avez des allumettes?
8. Vous avez des magazines?
9. Vous avez des crayons?
10. Vous avez des timbres?

E. COUNTING THE COST!

You have been shopping three times and have spent a lot of money! Afterwards you write a list to see exactly how much you have spent.

You have just done the first item on list Number 1. Now see if you can do all the calculations and work out the total cost of each shopping expedition.

1.
3 crayons à 0,60F — 1,80F
10 timbres à 1F —
1 sac à dos à 200F —
4 cartes postales à 1,40F —
2 paquets de cigarettes à 3,80F —
TOTAL —

2.
3 boîtes d'allumettes à 0,70F —
2 bouteilles de whisky à 50F —
1 livre à 10,30F —
1 magazine à 5,90F —
1 valise à 120F —
TOTAL —

3.
2 paquets de bonbons à 3,10F —
1 sac à main à 60F —
7 stylos à 0,80F —
1 paquet d'enveloppes à 1,20F —
2 journaux à 1,70F —
TOTAL —

F. NUMBERS

You will need these in order to understand the price of the different articles in a shop. Some of them you will probably know already.

1 – un	11 – onze	30 – trente
2 – deux	12 – douze	40 – quarante
3 – trois	13 – treize	50 – cinquante
4 – quatre	14 – quatorze	60 – soixante
5 – cinq	15 – quinze	70 – soixante-dix
6 – six	16 – seize	80 – quatre-vingts
7 – sept	17 – dix-sept	90 – quatre-vingt-dix
8 – huit	18 – dix-huit	100 – cent
9 – neuf	19 – dix-neuf	
10 – dix	20 – vingt	

G. ASKING THE PRICE

a. You want to know the price of the items shown in the pictures. How would you ask the questions?

b. Look at the prices on the articles and work out how you would say them in French.

Example

a. C'est combien les cigarettes?

b. Trois francs quatre-vingts.

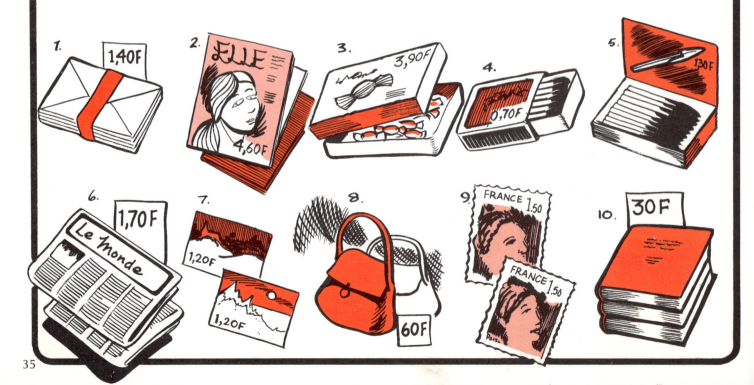

H. WHAT WOULD YOU SAY?

You should now be able to walk into a French shop and buy a few basic items. Here is a chance for you to test your skill! Imagine that you are the customer in these pictures and work out what you and the shopkeeper would say to each other.

I. STORY TIME
La première cigarette!
Part 1

Un jour Jacques dit à Mme Ragoût: 'Au revoir, maman! Je vais à la plage!'

Mais elle répond: 'Non, Jacques, va s'il te plaît au bureau de tabac!'

'Mais maman!' s'écrie Jacques.

Sa mère insiste: 'Je voudrais un journal, des enveloppes et des timbres. Achète-moi quatre timbres à un franc cinquante. Voilà neuf francs!'

Jacques sort de la tente et prend la direction de la rue. Juste en face du bloc sanitaire il rencontre son père.

'Où vas-tu, Jacques', demande M. Ragoût, 'à la piscine?'

'Non!' répond Jacques, irrité. 'Je vais au bureau de tabac pour maman!'

'Au bureau de tabac?' dit M. Ragoût. 'Parfait! Achète-moi un paquet de cigarettes – des Gitanes – et une boîte d'allumettes, s'il te plaît. Tu peux acheter des bonbons pour toi'.

'Oh, merci beaucoup!' dit Jacques avec une grimace.

M. Ragoût lui donne sept francs cinquante.

'Ah, les parents!' pense Jacques. 'Ils sont impossibles!'

Part 2

Jacques sort du camping et dix minutes après il arrive au bureau de tabac. Il y entre et achète tous les articles pour ses parents. Il achète aussi un paquet de nougat pour lui-même. Il quitte le bureau de tabac et descend la rue dans la direction du camping.

Soudain il a une idée! Il va derrière un arbre et

Questions

1. Where does Jacques want to go?
2. Where does Mme Ragoût want him to go?
3. What exactly does she ask him to get for her?
4. How much money does she give him?
5. Which way does he go?
6. Where does he meet his father?
7. Where does M. Ragoût think that Jacques is going?
8. How does Jacques feel about his father's question?
9. What does M. Ragoût ask Jacques to buy for him?
10. What does he say Jacques can buy for himself?
11. How much money does he give him?
12. What does Jacques think to himself?

ouvre le paquet de cigarettes. Avec une allumette il allume une cigarette et il commence à fumer – sa première cigarette! Après avoir fini la cigarette il continue vers le camping.

Mais en arrivant au camping il s'arrête à côté du bureau. Son visage devient pâle. Il souffre!

Il dit: 'Oh! J'ai mal à l'estomac! Vite, les toilettes!'

Il entre dans le bloc sanitaire et vomit dans un lavabo.

'Ah, les cigarettes! Je déteste les cigarettes!' pense Jacques.

Questions

1. How long does it take him to get to the shop?
2. What does he buy for himself?
3. Where does he go when he leaves the shop?
4. Where does he hide?
5. What does he do?
6. Has he ever done this before?
7. Where does he stop on reaching the campsite?
8. What happens to his face?
9. Where does he decide to make for?
10. What happens next?
11. What does he think to himself?

J. PRICE CHECK

You will find it a great help, when you are in France, if you can work out quickly how much French prices are in English money. The exact value of the franc and of the pound changes all the time of course, but here are two quick ways of working out approximately what French prices would be in pence or pounds.

1. Small amounts

| 1 Franc = 10p |

 3,20F

Example
This bottle of lemonade would cost about 32p.

For prices below ten francs **multiply** the number of francs by ten and this gives you the English value in **pence**.

N.B. You will notice that the French use a comma instead of a decimal point!

Now work out the following prices in English money:

2. Larger amounts

10 francs = £1

For prices of ten francs and over you have to **divide** the number of francs by ten. This time the answer you get will be the English value in **pounds**.

Example
This suitcase would cost about £22.

Now try your skill with the following prices:

1.

Employé: Bonjour madame, vous désirez?

2.

Mme Ragoût: Je voudrais aller à Paris, s'il vous plaît.

3.

Employé: Eh bien, prenez le train!

4.

Mme Ragoût: C'est combien un aller et retour pour Paris?

5.

Employé: Deux cent trente francs.

6.

Mme Ragoût: A quelle heure y a-t-il un train?

7.

Employé: A huit heures dix, onze heures trente et quinze heures quarante-cinq.

8.

Mme Ragoût: Merci beaucoup!

9.

Mme Ragoût: Oh!... Où est la gare, s'il vous plaît?

10.

Employé: Avenue Napoléon, en face de l'église!

11.

Mme Ragoût: Merci beaucoup monsieur, vous êtes très gentil!

12.

Employé: Je vous en prie, madame!

B. USEFUL WORDS

le train	la gare	un aller
le car	la gare routière	un aller et retour
le métro	la station de métro	
l'autobus	l'arrêt d'autobus	
le bateau	le port	
l'avion	l'aéroport	
{ l'aéroglisseur	l'hoverport	
{ l'hovercraft		

C. WHICH NUMBER?

You are at a coach station in a town in the North West of France. Various people come up to you and ask you which coach they should take to get to a number of different towns. Look at the pictures and work out the answers you would give them.

Example

Question: Le car pour Paris, s'il vous plaît?
Answer: Vingt-cinq!

1. Le car pour Boulogne, s'il vous plaît?
2. Le car pour Lille, s'il vous plaît?
3. Le car pour Dieppe, s'il vous plaît?
4. Le car pour Versailles, s'il vous plaît?
5. Le car pour Le Havre, s'il vous plaît?
6. Le car pour Dunkerque, s'il vous plaît?
7. Le car pour Calais, s'il vous plaît?
8. Le car pour Amiens, s'il vous plaît?
9. Le car pour Rouen, s'il vous plaît?
10. Le car pour Le Touquet, s'il vous plaît?

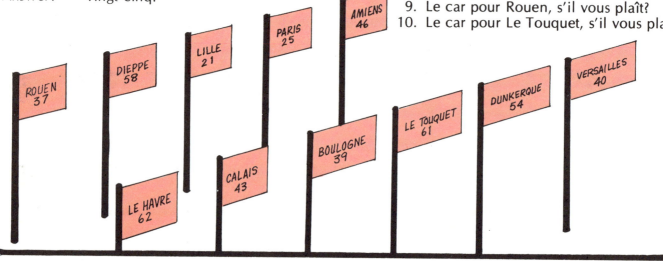

D. MORNING CLOCKS

These clocks all show times before midday.

a. Write down the times in figures using hours and minutes only.
b. Write out these times, in words, in French.

Example
a. 8.15
b. huit heures quinze

E. 24 HOUR CLOCKS

These digital clocks and watches all show times between midday and midnight according to the twenty-four-hour-clock system.

a. Work out **in French** in words the twenty-four-hour-clock version of the times as shown in the pictures.

b. Work out how we would describe these times **in English** in normal everyday language.

Example

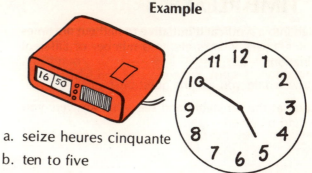

a. seize heures cinquante
b. ten to five

F. HOW MUCH?

Here you can see a number of tickets to different destinations.

a. Think out how you would ask how much each ticket costs.

b. Look at the price and see if you can work out what answer you would be given.

Example

a. C'est combien un aller pour Rouen?
b. Cinquante-cinq francs.

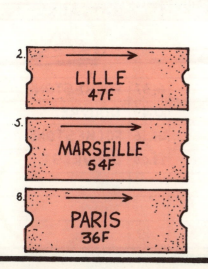
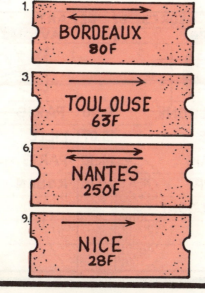
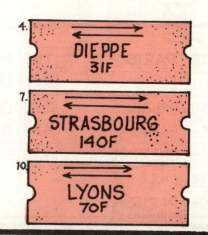

G. TIME PLEASE!

You go into a **syndicat d'initiative** to find out the times of trains, buses, planes etc. to a number of different destinations.

a. How would you ask the questions?

b. Look at the timetable and see what answers you would be given.

Example

a. A quelle heure y a-t-il un car pour Dieppe?

b. A seize heures trente-huit

H. WHAT WOULD YOU SAY?

Let's see if you could ask for travel information in a *syndicat d'initiative*. Work out the conversations suggested by the pictures, imagining that you are the tourist.

I. STORY TIME
L'héroïsme de Charles Dupont
Part 1

Charles Dupont est employé de banque. En général il quitte la banque à dix-sept heures trente. Mais aujourd'hui il a rendez-vous chez le dentiste à quinze heures vingt. Il déteste aller chez le dentiste! Il quitte la banque à quatorze heures trente. Il ferme la porte de la banque, regarde à droite et à gauche et traverse la rue. Pour aller chez le dentiste il prend l'autobus numéro quarante-deux. L'arrêt d'autobus est en face de la banque.

Questions

1. Where does Charles Dupont work?
2. At what time does he usually leave work?
3. Today is special – where is he going?
4. At what time is his appointment?
5. Is he looking forward to it?
6. At what time does he leave work today?
7. What does he do before crossing the road?
8. What is the number of the bus he must take?
9. Where is the bus-stop?

Part 2

Cinq minutes après une voiture arrive et s'arrête devant la banque. Mais, quelle horreur! Deux hommes masqués descendent de la voiture et entrent dans la banque. Ils portent des revolvers! Des voleurs qui attaquent la banque! Il faut téléphoner à la police!

A côté de l'arrêt d'autobus il y a une cabine téléphonique. Charles entre dans la cabine et compose le numéro. Après quinze secondes une femme répond.

Charles dit: 'Venez vite! Il y a des voleurs dans la banque, rue de l'Eglise! Ils sont armés!'

Il quitte la cabine téléphonique et se cache derrière un arbre.

Questions

1. How much time passes before the car arrives?
2. Where does it stop?
3. How does Charles know that the two men are robbers?
4. What does he realise he must do?
5. Where is the call-box?
6. What does Charles do in the call-box?
7. How long does he have to wait for an answer?
8. What street name does he give?
9. Where does he hide?

Part 3

Trois minutes après une voiture bleue et un petit autobus noir arrivent, et vingt agents de police en descendent. Quand les voleurs quittent la banque ils sont capturés par les agents et emmenés au commissariat.

Questions

1. How long does it take for the police to get there?
2. Describe the police vehicles.
3. How many policemen are there?
4. What happens when the robbers leave the bank?
5. Who thanks M. Dupont?
6. How does this person describe Charles?
7. What thought makes Charles very happy?
8. What thought makes him feel far from happy?

Le directeur de la banque dit: 'Merci beaucoup M. Dupont. Vous êtes un héros!'

Charles Dupont est très content. Il imagine sa photo dans le journal – à la première page! Mais soudain il pense: 'Le dentiste! Zut alors!'

Est-il content maintenant? Oh non!

J. FIND OUT FOR YOURSELF

Here is a quiz about transport in France. You may know some of the answers already. Try and find the remaining answers by asking people who have been to France or by looking in books on France in your school or local library. A French dictionary will help you understand the meaning of the signs.

For each question you are given three possible answers of which only one is correct.

1. France's most modern airport is at Roissy, twenty two kilometres north of Paris. It was opened in 1974 and has been designed to handle twenty-two million passengers a year. What is it called?
    a. Orly.
    b. Le Bourget.
    c. Charles de Gaulle.

2. This is one of the few road signs that are very common in France but are not seen in this country. What does it stand for?
   a. The road to Tourville is closed.
   b. You are just leaving the town of Tourville.
   c. You are just entering the town of Tourville.

3. The Citroën 2 CV – one of the most popular cars ever produced by the French motor industry. It is very basic but cheap, economical and tough. What does 2 CV mean?
   a. 2 horse power.
   b. 2 c.c.
   c. 2 door.

4. **Le Mistral** – one of France's most famous express trains. It is a luxury train and so it only has first class carriages. There are facilities for passengers to have their hair cut, go shopping in a boutique, hire a secretary or make a phone-call. Which French cities does it connect?
   a. Paris–Bordeaux.
   b. Paris–Marseille–Nice.
   c. Paris–Strasbourg.

5 This is a French motorway sign. The French were slow to build motorways at first, but in recent years an extensive network has been constructed at amazing speed. They are excellent roads, but there is one drawback indicated by the word **péage** on the sign. What does it mean?
   a. Delays caused by roadworks.
   b. You have to pay a toll charge.
   c. Speed restrictions in force.

UNIT SIX — AU CAFÉ 1

A. DIALOGUE

Monique and Jacques have been to the beach for a swim. On their way back to the campsite they call in at the Café de la Plage for a drink. Monique is feeling generous and offers to treat her brother. Jacques does not refuse!

1.

Garçon: Qu'est-ce que vous prenez, mademoiselle?

2.

Monique: Je voudrais un café, s'il vous plaît.

3.

Garçon: Un café crème?

4.

Monique: Non, je n'aime pas le café crème!

5.

Monique: Un café noir, s'il vous plaît.

6.

Monique: Et je voudrais aussi une limonade.

7.

Garçon: Bien, mademoiselle, c'est tout?
Monique: Oui, merci, c'est tout.

8.

(*The waiter returns a few minutes later with the order.*)

9.

Garçon: Voilà, mademoiselle! Un café noir et une limonade!

10.

Monique: Merci, monsieur. L'addition, s'il vous plaît.

11.

Garçon: Voilà, mademoiselle, quatre francs vingt.

12.

Monique: Quatre francs vingt... voilà, monsieur!
Garçon: Merci, mademoiselle!

B. USEFUL WORDS

un café crème
un café noir
un thé au lait
un thé au citron
un chocolat chaud
un chocolat froid

une bière
un vin rouge
un vin blanc
un vin rosé

un jus d'ananas
un jus de pamplemousse
un jus d'orange
une limonade
une orangeade
un coca cola

C. FANCY A DRINK?

The people in the pictures are offering you a number of different drinks. In each case work out the **two** possible answers.

a. Accepting the drink because you like it.
b. Refusing the drink because you do not like it.

Example

un vin rouge?

a. Oui, merci, j'aime le vin rouge.
b. Non, merci, je n'aime pas le vin rouge.

1. un café noir?
2. un thé au lait?
3. une bière?
4. un vin rosé?
5. une orangeade?
6. un chocolat froid?
7. un jus de pamplemousse?
8. un coca cola?
9. une limonade?
10. un vin blanc?

E. LIKES AND DISLIKES

a. Make a list of all the things you like to drink. Each one should start: **'J'aime . . . .'**
b. Make another list, this time of the things you do not like to drink. You should begin each one with: **'Je n'aime pas . . . .'**

F. DO YOU LIKE?

How would you ask someone if they like the drinks shown in the pictures?

Example

Vous aimez le chocolat?

1.
2.
3.
4.
5.
6.
7.
8.
9.
10.

G. ANSWERS PLEASE!

Answer in French these questions about your own likes and dislikes. Tell the truth!

Example

Question: Vous aimez le café noir?
Answer: Oui, j'aime le café noir.
or: Non, je n'aime pas le café noir.

1. Vous aimez le thé au lait?
2. Vous aimez le coca cola?
3. Vous aimez le jus de pamplemousse?
4. Vous aimez le chocolat chaud?
5. Vous aimez le café crème?
6. Vous aimez le jus d'ananas?
7. Vous aimez l'orangeade?
8. Vous aimez le chocolat froid?
9. Vous aimez le jus d'orange?
10. Vous aimez la limonade?

Café de la Gare

Thé 2,90F
Chocolat 2,90F
Café 1,40F
Bière 2,70F
Vins 1,70F

chocolat froid ......?
vin rouge ......?
...?...?

Café de la Gare

chocolat froid 2,90F
vin rouge 1,70F
service 12% 0,55F
―――――――
5,15F

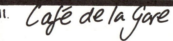

I. STORY TIME
L'importance du chocolat
Part 1

Il est onze heures vingt-cinq. L'inspecteur Leflic gare sa voiture à côté d'une petite boulangerie. Il touche sa poche – oui, son revolver est là. Cette fois c'est une mission très dangereuse! Il cherche le célèbre gangster Pierre Tapefort, qui a déjà

Questions

1. What time is it?
2. Where does Inspector Leflic park his car?
3. Why does he touch his pocket?
4. Who is Pierre Tapefort?
5. What is his record?

assassiné deux employés de banque et un agent de police!

C'est aussi une mission très difficile. Tapefort est un homme intelligent et il est toujours déguisé – par exemple en journaliste, en chauffeur de taxi, en garçon de café, même en femme! Mais la police a reçu des informations importantes sur Pierre Tapefort. Il aime les omelettes et le chocolat froid. Il fréquente aussi un petit café en face de la gare routière.

Voilà le café, à côté du syndicat d'initiative! L'inspecteur traverse la rue et entre dans le café. Il trouve une table à gauche de la porte. Il commande un café crème et il observe les autres clients.

6. Why is this a difficult mission?
7. List some of Pierre Tapefort's disguises.
8. What does he like to eat and drink?
9. Describe the position of the café.
10. Where does Inspector Leflic sit when he enters the café?
11. What does he order?

Part 2

Un touriste entre et crie, avec un accent américain: 'Garçon! Garçon!'

Le garçon arrive et le touriste dit: 'Une omelette, s'il vous plaît! Et je voudrais aussi un chocolat.'

Leflic regarde le touriste américain avec intérêt. Une omelette et un chocolat! C'est peut-être le criminel!

Le garçon demande: 'Un chocolat froid?'

'Non!' répond le touriste, 'Un chocolat chaud, s'il vous plaît.'

'Mais non!' pense M. Leflic. 'Ce n'est pas mon

homme. Tapefort aime le chocolat froid!'

Une femme entre et s'assied à une table à côté du bar. Immédiatement le garçon place quelque chose sur la table.

'C'est curieux ça!' pense Leflic. 'Qui est cette femme?'

Leflic quitte sa table et traverse le café pour aller aux toilettes. Il passe à côté de la table de la femme. Elle mange une omelette et elle boit un chocolat froid!

'C'est Tapefort!' pense Leflic. 'Cette femme est en réalité le criminel Pierre Tapefort déguisé en femme!'

Questions

1. Who comes into the café?
2. What does this person order?
3. Why is Leflic interested in this person?
4. Why is Leflic disappointed?
5. Where does the lady sit?
6. Does she have to wait before being served?
7. What does the Inspector do?
8. How does Leflic manage to see what she is eating?
9. What is she eating and drinking?
10. What does the Inspector think?

Part 3

Dans les toilettes Leflic sort le revolver de sa poche. Il ouvre la porte et il avance vite vers la femme. Il dit: 'C'est la police, Tapefort! Inutile de résister!'

Questions

1. What does Leflic do before opening the door to come back into the room?
2. What does he say to the lady?
3. Describe her reactions.
4. Who is the lady?
5. What does the inspector think to himself?
6. What does he say to the lady?
7. What does he do when he leaves the cafe?
8. Where does Leflic find the letter?
9. What does the letter say?
10. What does Leflic now realise?

La femme devient pâle et pousse un cri de terreur. Le garçon arrive et crie: 'Mais monsieur, ce n'est pas un criminel! C'est ma femme, Mme Duclos!'

'Mon Dieu!' pense Leflic, 'J'ai fait une erreur! Ce n'est pas Tapefort! C'est vraiment une femme!'

Les clients regardent l'inspecteur Leflic qui devient rouge et répète: 'Oh pardon madame, pardon, c'est une erreur!'

Vite il quitte le café et traverse la rue pour retourner à sa voiture. Sur la voiture il trouve une petite lettre: 'J'aime le chocolat froid, mais j'adore le chocolat chaud!' La lettre était signée 'P.T.'

'Zut alors!' dit Leflic. 'Tapefort, c'était le touriste américain!'

J. FIND OUT FOR YOURSELF

The questions in this quiz all have something to do with French drinks, both alcoholic and non-alcoholic. You should be able to find the answers in an encyclopaedia or in books about France. A French dictionary should give you the answers to questions 2 and 5. Another possibility is to ask a person who is fond of a glass of French wine – there are quite a lot of them about!

For each question you are given three possible answers of which only one is correct.

1. After wine, coffee is the French national drink. It is drunk at any time of the day, but especially for breakfast and after meals. How is it usually drunk at breakfast time?
   a. Black, in a small cup.
   b. From a bowl with plenty of milk.
   c. In a normal-sized cup with a little cream or milk.

2. The French drink fruit syrups where in this country we drink squash. These syrups are sold in tins or bottles. They are diluted with water like squash but are very sweet and taste quite different. A favourite flavour is **grenadine**. What fruit is it made from?
   a. Pears.
   b. Grapes.
   c. Pomegranates.

3. These two alcoholic drinks are made from apples. The one of course is cider and the other is **calvados** a strong white brandy. Not surprisingly they are both produced in a region that is known for its apples. Which of the following is it?
   a. Brittany.
   b. Normandy.
   c. Provence.

4. This is the monastery near Grenoble where, centuries ago, one of France's most famous liqueurs was invented. The secret recipe is still held by the monks. It is flavoured with 130 different plants gathered high up in the mountains of the French Alps. What is the name of the liqueur?
   a. Cointreau.
   b. Chartreuse.
   c. Chablis.

5. A popular soft drink, which is very refreshing on a hot day, is made by squeezing the juice from a fresh lemon. You add your own water and you can put in sugar if you wish. What is this drink called?
   a. Limonade.
   b. Jus de citron.
   c. Citron pressé.